P9-BZU-358

The Birthday Present

tiger tales

Little Monkey was very excited. It was Mommy Monkey's birthday and he had found her a juicy mango. He decided to hide it under a bush until Mommy Monkey got back.

Little Monkey climbed a tree to wait for Mommy Monkey. He had almost reached the top when he saw Little Elephant.

He bounced onto Little Elephant's
head and slid down his trunk. It was
so much fun that he did it again, and
again, faster and faster!

But he landed in the bush, and . . .

SPLAT!

He squashed Mommy Monkey's lovely ripe mango!

"Don't worry," said Little Elephant. "Let's go back to the tree you picked it from."

So they set off for the mango tree.

But when they arrived they found someone had picked all the fruit!

"Oh no!" cried Little Monkey. "I have to find another mango before Mommy gets back."

Just then Little Parrot flew by. "If you're looking for mangoes," she said, "there's a tree on the other side of the river."

When they reached the river, they saw Little Tiger splashing in the water.

"Have you come to play with me?" he asked.

"Not today," said Little Monkey. "We're looking for a birthday present."

Little Elephant splashed
through the water with
Little Monkey on his back.

When they reached
e other side, they
w the mango tree.
ttle Monkey
rambled up the tree
d picked the biggest
ango he could see.
But as he was
imbing back down . . .

he heard an angry shout.
"That's my tree," said a large monkey.
"Give me back that mango!"

021184

Little Monkey leaped onto Little Elephant's back, carrying the mango.

"Hurry!" shouted Little Monkey.

Little Elephant splashed into the river, with Little Monkey clinging tightly to his ears.

The large monkey couldn't follow them through the water.

"That was close!" said Little Elephant.

They hurried home through the jungle, and
Little Monkey put the heavy mango down.
But just at that moment . . .

Mommy Monkey arrived home. She was so pleased to see Little Monkey that she didn't notice the lovely ripe mango lying on the ground.

"Look out!" shouted Little Monkey.

Just in time, he rolled the mango to safety.

"Nice save!" Mommy Monkey exclaimed.

"Happy Birthday, Mommy!" said Little Monkey. "Perhaps you should eat it right away, before anything else happens to it!"

Little Tiger character taken from the series of books
by Julie Sykes and Tim Warnes
Illustrated by Czes Pachela, based on
the characters created by Tim Warnes

tiger tales
an imprint of ME Media LLC
202 Old Ridgefield Road
Wilton, CT 06897
First Published in Great Britain 2001
by Little Tiger Press, London
© 2001 Little Tiger Press
Printed in Singapore
ISBN 1-58925-363-9